THE WORLD OF NASCAR

BUILDING A STOCK CAR:
The Need for More Speed

T R A D I T I O N B O O K S™
EXCELSIOR, MINNESOTA

BY WILL DeBOARD

Published by **Tradition Books**™ and distributed to the
school and library market by **The Child's World**®
P.O. Box 326
Chanhassen, MN 55317-0326
800/599-READ
http://www.childsworld.com

Photo Credits
Cover and title page: Courtesy Dodge Motorsports
Allsport: 6 (Adam Pretty); 12 (Mark Thompson)
AP/Wide World: 5, 22 (top), 28
Dodge Motorsports: 8, 10, 16
HowStuffWorks.com: 9, 15
Sports Gallery: 11, 14, 18, 21 (Brian Cleary); 17, 19, 20, 27 (Joe
  Robbins); 22 bottom, 24, 25, 26, 29 (Al Messerschmidt)

Book production by Shoreline Publishing Group, LLC
Art direction and design by The Design Lab

Library of Congress Cataloging-in-Publication Data

DeBoard, Will.
  Building a stock car : the need for more speed / by Will DeBoard.
     p. cm. — (The world of NASCAR series)
Includes index.
Summary: Examines the design and purpose of the different parts of stock cars and describes
how to construct them.
  ISBN 1-59187-000-3 (Library bound : alk. paper)
  1. Stock cars (Automobiles)—Design and construction—Juvenile literature. [1. Stock cars
(Automobiles)—Design and construction.] I. Title. II. Series.
  TL236.28 .D43 2002
  629.228—dc21   2002004639

BUILDING A STOCK CAR

Table of Contents

I N T R O D U C T I O N

They've Come a Long Way

S tock car racing has come a long way. In the early days of the sport, the cars were "strictly stock." That means that most of them were driven right off the street to the race track. Almost nobody had a car that was made just to race. The drivers were often also the car's mechanics. They tinkered and tweaked their cars to get the best performance.

Now, take a trip forward to 2001. The racing action is still fast and furious, but the cars are very different. Today, builders create special models of passenger cars for use in NASCAR racing. Since 1948, NASCAR has been the highest level of stock car racing. NASCAR stands for National Association for Stock Car Automobile Racing. In 2001, there were four different types

of car models that raced on the NASCAR's top-level Winston
Cup circuit. Those were the Chevrolet Monte Carlo, the Ford
Taurus, the Pontiac Grand Prix, and the Dodge Intrepid.

You might see cars with those names and those basic
shapes on the road in your town. But even though they look
similar, the cars you see racing don't come close to regular cars.
It's not like the old days. Drivers don't take the family car out to
the track on the weekend. Today, stock car racing is a big business. Every team is trying to get the most out of their cars to

By 1969, star driver Richard Petty's stock car
still looked much like a passenger car—but with
a powerful engine.

win the race. Winning means glory, and also big money.

How are today's stock cars designed and built? It takes engineering, computers, steel, rubber, and lots of hard work by many people. From the first step to the last, it takes months for a car to be ready for race day.

A lot of things have changed since those early days of stock cars. One thing has remained the same, however. Drivers and their teams spend all their time and energy trying to make their cars go faster!

The Dodge Intrepid is one of the cars today's NASCAR drivers use. It was designed for one thing: speed.

Framing a Car

The **chassis** (CHA-see) is the steel framework of the car. You won't see any part of the chassis on a completed car. It's under the colorful body. The chassis's main jobs are to keep the car together and the driver safe.

Because NASCAR rules are very strict, most team's chassis are similar. This keeps the competition fair. There are several companies whose only business is to build chassis for stock car racing. Some teams, especially those with more money, can build chassis in their own garages. This is quite different from the cars you see on the road, where assembly-line machines spit out car after car. NASCAR stock cars are hand-assembled at nearly every stage, with lots of help from computers.

Until the 1960s, stock cars used in racing were bought from regular auto sales lots. They were then modified in the

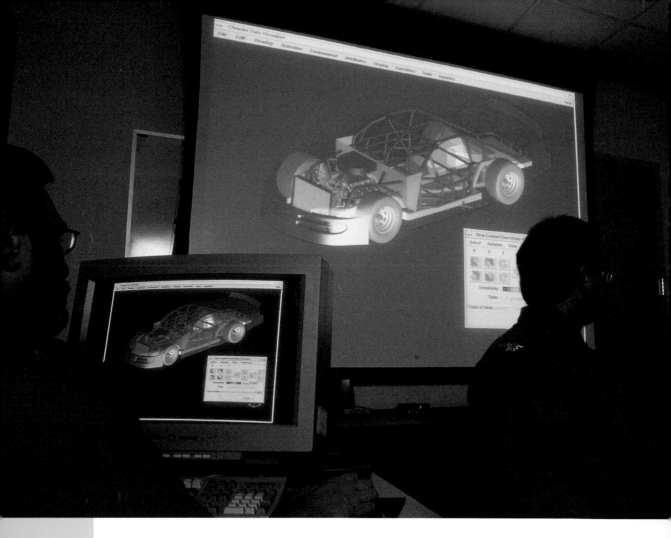

racer's garage. Today's cars are much different, and that

begins with the chassis.

Crew chiefs, who lead race teams, take careful notes

while a chassis is being prepared. These notes help ensure

that every chassis a team makes is the same. The tool used to

do that job is called the **jig.** The jig, also called a building fix-

ture, is used to hold the chassis pieces together while they are

The first step to Victory Lane is taken with a
computer. Designers put together the whole car
on screen first.

being welded. This guarantees every piece will be built the same as the last one.

The most important part of the chassis is the **roll cage.** When the driver is racing, he is surrounded by the steel of the roll cage. This steel protects him during an accident or crash. The roll cage is made of the strongest steel and will not crumple under pressure.

Guided by computer design, craftspeople put together the chassis, the steel skeleton of the car.

Every piece of the chassis is welded to each other piece by hand. Thick steel tubes are carefully arranged to form the shape. The end result looks like the skeleton of a car. You can see the basic shape, but you can also see right through it.

Next, there are several other pieces to the puzzle. After the chassis has been welded together, several pieces are attached to the car. These parts are made of thinner sheet metal and include the fender wells, floor pan, and firewall.

This computer model shows how the engine rests in the front and the body covers the chassis.

THE OTHER RACE CARS

What's the difference between the cars of NASCAR and those of other racing organizations? The answer is quite a lot.

NASCAR's cars look different than Formula One (F1), Championship Auto Racing Teams (CART), and Indy Racing League (IRL) cars. The F1, CART, and IRL cars are all called open-wheel cars (above). This means they don't have fenders. Also, in all three cases, the driver isn't encased in a roll cage. The shape of these cars is longer and more tube-shaped.

NASCAR cars also don't go quite as fast as these other cars. Most NASCAR races are also held on oval tracks. On these, drivers only make left turns. NASCAR races only twice a year on road courses. The other organizations almost always race on road courses with many left and right turns.

Computers also play an even bigger role in the designing of the open-wheel cars. NASCAR shops spend more time trying to improve their car's performance by trial and error.

The fender wells form the spaces where the tires will be placed. The floor pan covers the underside of the car. The firewall goes between the engine compartment and the driver. The thick plate protects the driver from the searing heat of the engine.

At this point in the construction process, every car is nearly the same. It doesn't matter if it's a Chevrolet, Dodge, Pontiac, or Ford. They all look the same now. The next step really starts to make each car unique.

The fenders used on stock cars take a real beating, as this post-race photo shows.

C H A P T E R   T W O

Car Bodies

When the body is attached, stock cars begin to look different from each other. The body is mainly made up of standard sheet metal. It is handmade by special workers called **body fabricators.** After selecting a flat piece of sheet metal, the body fabricator lays a **template** directly onto it. He then traces around the template's edges with a marker.

The body fabricator uses several types of metal shears to cut the shape from the metal. The piece of metal will then be curved and molded to form the shape of the car. This is one of the most difficult parts of constructing the body. The cut metal is put through two gigantic rollers. As it goes through this machine, the fabricator bends the piece to fit. The piece is then mounted to the car. If it doesn't fit, then the piece

might have to be reshaped. Sometimes, the fabricator will have to cut a whole new piece.

When the piece finally does fit, holes will be drilled to insert rivets. These rivets are used to attach the metal panels to the chassis. In some cases, there may be as many as a hundred holes in one piece of sheet metal. Stock cars go through intense pounding, so the pieces must be tightly attached.

Once all the rivets are secured, then the body pieces are welded together. The body should be one continuous piece

Welders join the shaped pieces of metal one by one.
Rivets are also used to keep the body together.

with no visible seams or cracks. The entire body is smooth, too. This is important to help the car cut through the air smoothly and with little resistance. It may take days, even weeks, to get the body as smooth as possible. When the car is traveling at its top speed, even the smallest bump or crack can affect its speed.

Once the body is completely smooth, it is painted with a gray primer to prevent rust. Once the primer is applied, the interior parts will be fitted into the chassis. These parts include the dashboard and the car seat.

Ready for the paint shop: This body has been fully assembled and polished smooth for the best air flow.

Each seat is custom fitted to each driver's body to ensure maximum comfort. There is very little padding such as you would see in a passenger car. As the driver looks around inside the car, he can see the steel tubes of the roll cage. There is nothing else between him and the body of the car.

With the body in good shape, it's time to go under the car. Coming into the garage next are the brakes and the **suspension** system.

Along with computers, engineers use smaller models of the car to test their designs in wind tunnels.

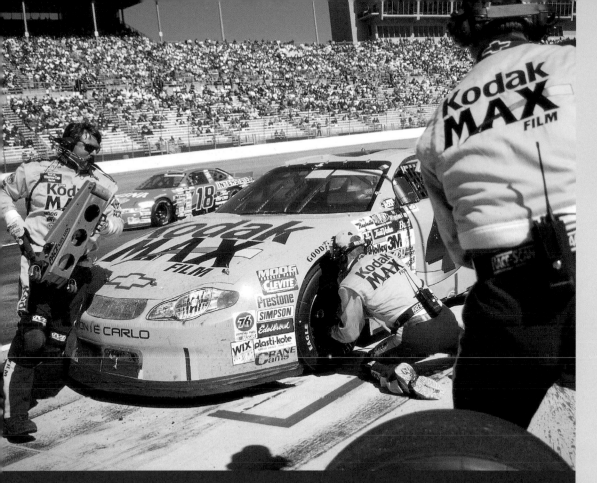

NOT YOUR AVERAGE FAMILY CAR

At first glance, a NASCAR Chevrolet Monte Carlo and the Monte Carlo you see on the street look similar. If you take a second look, though, the similarities end.

NASCAR cars have no doors or windows. The drivers climb in through the window opening. A NASCAR car also has no passenger seat or back seat. These cars aren't built for passengers. There isn't much comfort for the driver either, but the custom-built seat helps.

There are no lights on a NASCAR car, either. Stickers on the front of the car make it look like there are lights, but those are just for show. There is also no air conditioning, heater, stereo, cruise control, glove compartment, or horn. Stock cars are built to race, and anything that doesn't help them move faster won't be there.

Your lights are on! Oh, wait, those are just stickers. Check out all the other stickers on a typical stock car, too.

CHAPTER THREE

Suspension and Setup

After the primer has been painted, one of the next steps will be to attach the **suspension** underneath the car. The suspension is the system of springs and shock absorbers that affects how the car handles. This system is attached to the tires and axles.

The suspension won't make the car faster. In fact, most cars on a NASCAR track have similar top speeds. The suspension does help the car make it through turns faster. Every NASCAR driver and team says the handling of the car is what makes a winner.

Here's a good look at how a shock absorber, the silver tube, is a part of every one of the car's wheels.

Because every track on the
circuit is unique, every track
needs a different **setup** for
the suspension. The setup
means the way that each team
tightens or loosens parts of the
car to improve performance.
In some cases, crews will
make hundreds of changes to
the setup in the week between
races.

The first change to be made in a car's setup is tire air

pressure. Tires are changed during pit stops in a race. The air

pressure can be changed even before the driver makes that

stop. The driver is constantly in radio contact with his crew

chief. He lets his chief know how the car is handling on the

track. The chief is the one who then makes the decision

regarding air pressure. He directs the crew to prepare the new

**Adjusting tire pressure is one of the key ways that
race teams create the unique setup for their car.**

tires a certain way. Also, because air expands as it gets hotter, tires tend to expand during a race. Crew chiefs have to bear that in mind as well.

Different shock absorbers are also used for each track. Each driver has his own preference when it comes to how a car handles. Shock absorbers have a lot to do with that. For every bump the car drives over, the shock absorber will compress so the driver doesn't feel the bump. At 20 miles per hour (32 kilometers per hour), a bump isn't that bad. But at 175 miles per hour (281 kilometers per hour), a bump could throw him against the roof of his car if he isn't wearing a seat belt.

Attached to each wheel is a spring. It aids the shock absorber and keeps the ride even smoother. The tightness of

This car flies over a bump at Sears Point, a road course. These racetracks create the need for stronger shocks.

STEERING AND BRAKES

Two other features help the handling of the car: steering and brakes.

The steering wheel (top) is removable to help the driver get into the car more easily. Sometimes you see drivers before a race carrying their steering wheels.

Drivers use the same type of steering wheels at most tracks. Different brakes, however, are used for different tracks. At the longer tracks, brakes are rarely used. At big tracks, the brakes are only used to slow the car for pit stops, so a lighter system is used (bottom). At road courses and shorter tracks, the brakes are vital to success. There, the brakes are used several times during each lap. Considering the car is moving faster than 100 miles per hour (161 kilometers per hour) through these turns, the brakes need to be heavy-duty.

They also need to be cooled off more often. The friction of braking heats up the brakes so much that you can see them glow red-hot. Some teams will build three extra cooling hoses just for the brakes in these races. These hoses provide liquid for the brakes to cool them.

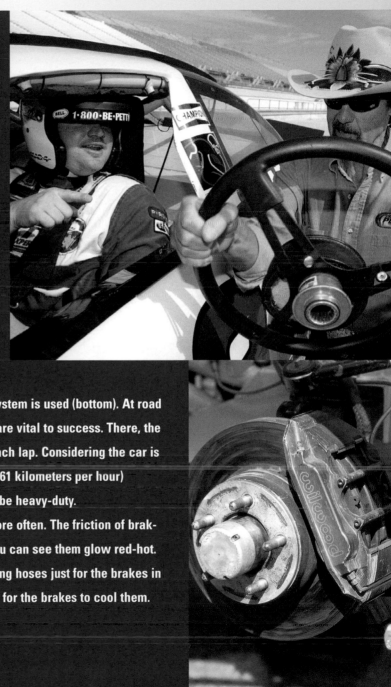

the springs greatly affects how the car handles. Tightening or loosening springs is another way teams set up a car.

Drivers have their own vocabulary when it comes to the car's handling. A "loose" car wiggles back and forth as it enters a turn. A "tight" car isn't turning enough when it goes into a turn. Springs can be adjusted to stop these handling problems.

The last piece of the suspension in the setup is the sway bar. As the car goes into each turn, it wants to roll toward the outside of the track. If you've ever been in a larger car, like a van, you can feel that roll. The sway bar keeps the car from rolling too far to the outside. It can also be adjusted before the race for each driver's needs.

A lot of work goes into setting up a car's suspension. The slightest improvement in a car's handling can mean the difference between winning and losing.

A car's setup helps drivers when they steer into a turn like this one.

C H A P T E R   F O U R

Vrrooom!

The final piece to be attached to a stock car is the engine. You would think it is the most important part of the car, but that isn't always the case. Because NASCAR has so many rules to ensure fairness, most teams' engines are very close in **horsepower.**

Each major American car builder with vehicles on the NASCAR circuit also has a racing division. That division is devoted to nothing but building engines for race cars. The quest for every team is to gain more horsepower from their engines.

A passenger car engine usually generates about 200 horsepower. That's more than enough to power you and your family on the highway. A stock car engine, on the other hand, generates about 750 horsepower. That's nearly four times more powerful than your family car.

With all this power, one of the biggest concerns in a long race is keeping the engine cool. The speed in these races can cause the engine to overheat easily. The main cooling system is a combination of oil and water that runs in tubes throughout the entire engine. Because of the very high temperatures, only high-strength hoses are used in the engine. Any time a hose fails on the track, it usually means two things. One is that there is suddenly a wet spot on the track that might cause a major wreck. The other is that the engine will usually overheat, ending that driver's race.

Oil also keeps other parts of the car cool. It runs throughout the entire body of the car thanks to a high-pressure pump. Because the oil flows through the entire engine and body,

It would take about 750 horses to equal the power of this engine.

nearly 18 quarts (17 liters) are used. Regular cars rarely use more than 5 quarts (4.73 liters).

A small radiator is in place to do nothing but cool the oil. The radiator is mounted in the left front of the car. The air rushing through during the race cools the oil. This is why teams scrub clean the outside grille of the car during pit stops. That keeps the air flowing freely.

Instead of a regular gas tank, race cars use **fuel cells.** Fuel cells are made of high-grade plastic that is very hard to

See how the engine fits into the chassis. Compare this to the computer drawing on page 10.

puncture or break. The cell also has many separate compart-
ments. If there is a puncture in one, only a small amount of
fuel will pour out. Otherwise, a puncture might empty the
car's entire supply.

Unlike **production cars,** race cars aren't started with
a key. Stock cars use a push-button system. Push the button
and the car immediately starts.

The **drivetrain** includes the car's clutch and transmission. The clutch is a device used to shift gears on the car.
Gears help an engine go faster or slower. Most race car drivers
don't use their clutch very often. Their clutches are designed
so a car can stay in fourth gear—its highest gear—all the way

Filling up the tank? Nope, filling up the fuel cells.
Pit crews can put 22 gallons of fuel into a car in
about 10 seconds.

around the track. Only on NASCAR's two road courses are

clutches used often during a race. On longer oval tracks, the

only time gears are shifted by the driver is when he enters

and leaves the pit area.

Now the car is ready to race. The chassis has been assem-

bled. The body has been carefully shaped. The suspension has

been carefully set up. The engine, brakes, and steering are

ready to roll.

Guess what? After each race, the team does it all over

again. That's right; they build a new race car each weekend

during the NASCAR season. While the chassis and body may

remain, the suspension and engine will be changed for every

To get from race to race, NASCAR teams haul their cars and equipment in these giant 18-wheelers.

race. Each team brings several of these cars to each race, ready for any emergency.

During each NASCAR weekend, there are really two races. The one everybody sees happens out on the track. That race is between drivers using their skill and daring to try to cross the finish line first.

The other race is between dedicated teams of hard-working experts. In garages across the country, they work long hours to create their racing machines. They try every week to get a little more power here, a little more steering ability there. If the guys at the shops aren't successful, it would take a miracle for their drivers to win. When they do win, however, everyone shares in the glory.

Here's the point of all this hard work: Watching your team cross the finish line first.

LOTS OF ENGINES!

Race teams bring as many as seven engines to each race. With each engine costing about $75,000, that's an expensive pile of metal.

Each engine they bring has its own special job. The qualifying engine is made with lighter parts than a race engine, because a car only takes one or two laps to qualify for the race. Those lighter parts may add one or two horsepower to the engine, and they probably won't break with only a few laps to race.

A practice engine is usually similar to a race engine. It is used during practice sessions so drivers and crew chiefs can figure out the suspension setup. They don't use their main race engine during practice because they want it to be fresh for the race.

The race engine itself is made with heavy-duty parts because it goes through a lot of stress during a race. After a race, the crew goes over each engine carefully and replaces any part that looks worn. It takes several days for a crew to make an engine ready for the next race.

GLOSSARY

body fabricators—specialized workers whose job is to construct the body of the car by hand

chassis—the steel framework of the car

crew chiefs—the leaders of race teams, they supervise team employees and are in charge on race day. They're responsible for race day changes and strategies.

drivetrain—the parts of the car—engine, transmission, axles—that link up to turn the wheels

fuel cells—specialized plastic tanks that each stock car uses instead of a single metal gas tank.

horsepower—the unit of measurement by which motors are measured; one horsepower is what it takes to lift 550 pounds (250 kilograms) 1foot (.3 meters) high in 1 second.

jig—the tool used to measure each piece of the chassis before it is welded together to ensure accurate fit

production cars—cars that roll off assembly lines for public use

roll cage—the frame of steel that protects the driver in accidents

setup—the way a car is prepared for a race

suspension—the system of shock absorbers, springs, and sway bars that affects the handling of the car

template—pieces of metal that are used to shape pieces of the body; templates are placed over sheet metal, and the metal is then cut to that exact size

FOR MORE INFORMATION ABOUT STOCK CARS

Books

Center, Bill. *Ultimate Stock Car*. New York: DK Publishing, 2000.

Gilden, Mel. *How They Work: NASCAR*. New York: William Morrow, 2000.

Parsons, Benny. *Inside Track: A Photo Documentary of NASCAR Stock Car Racing*. New York: Artisan Publishing, 1996.

Web Sites

The Official NASCAR Web Site
http://www.nascar.com
For an overview of an entire season of NASCAR as well as the history of the sport and a dictionary of racing terms

That's Racin'
http://www.thatsracin.com
The *Charlotte* (North Carolina) *Observer* newspaper's site is great for fans who want to read about their favorite drivers

INDEX

ABOUT THE AUTHOR

Will DeBoard lives in Modesto, California, with his wife, Paula, and two cats. He has covered motor sports for the *Modesto Bee* newspaper for six years. He has written articles about NASCAR, lower levels of stock car racing, Indy cars, and Formula 1. This is his first book.